THIS ADULT COLORING BOOK BELONGS TO:

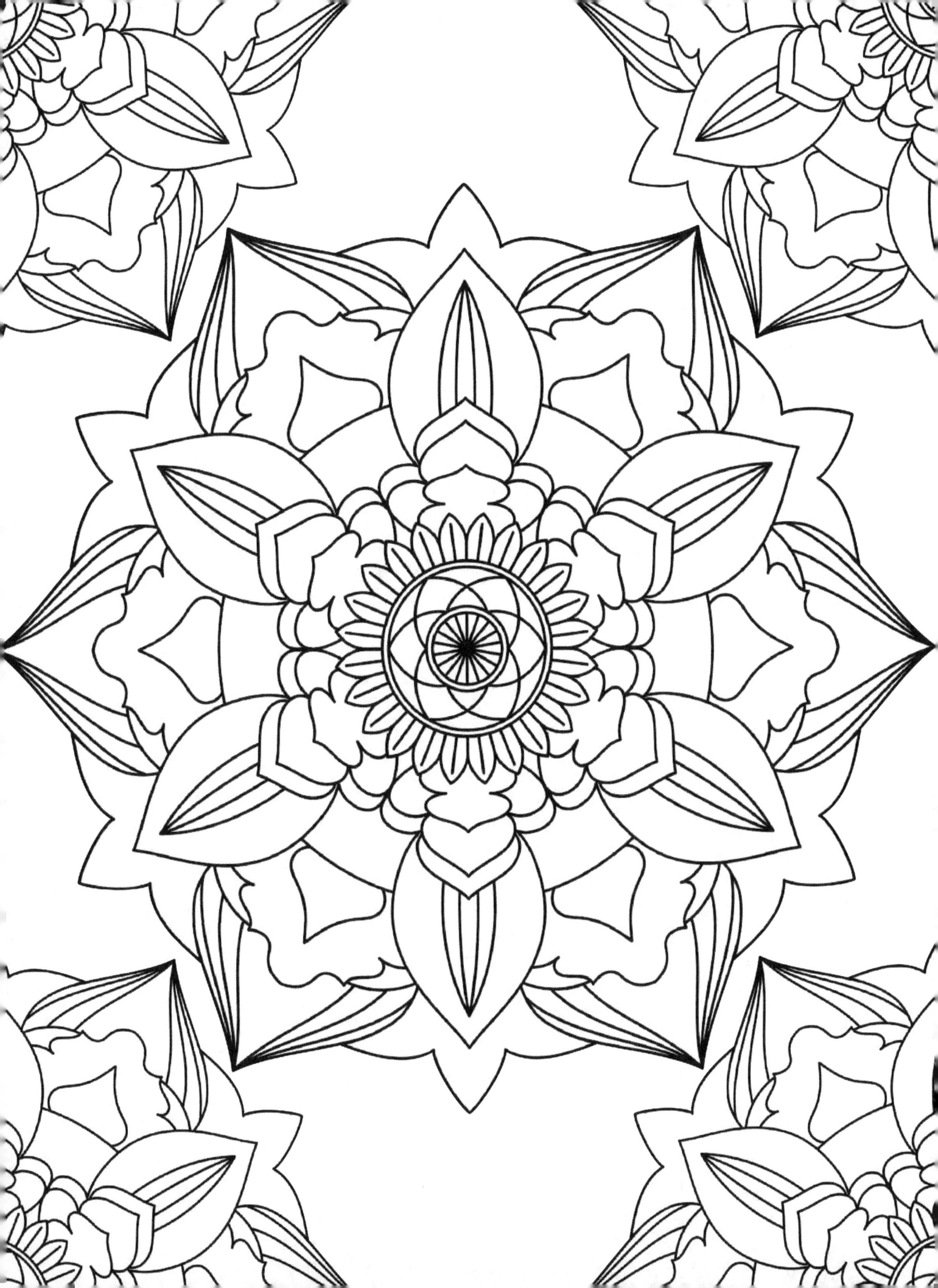

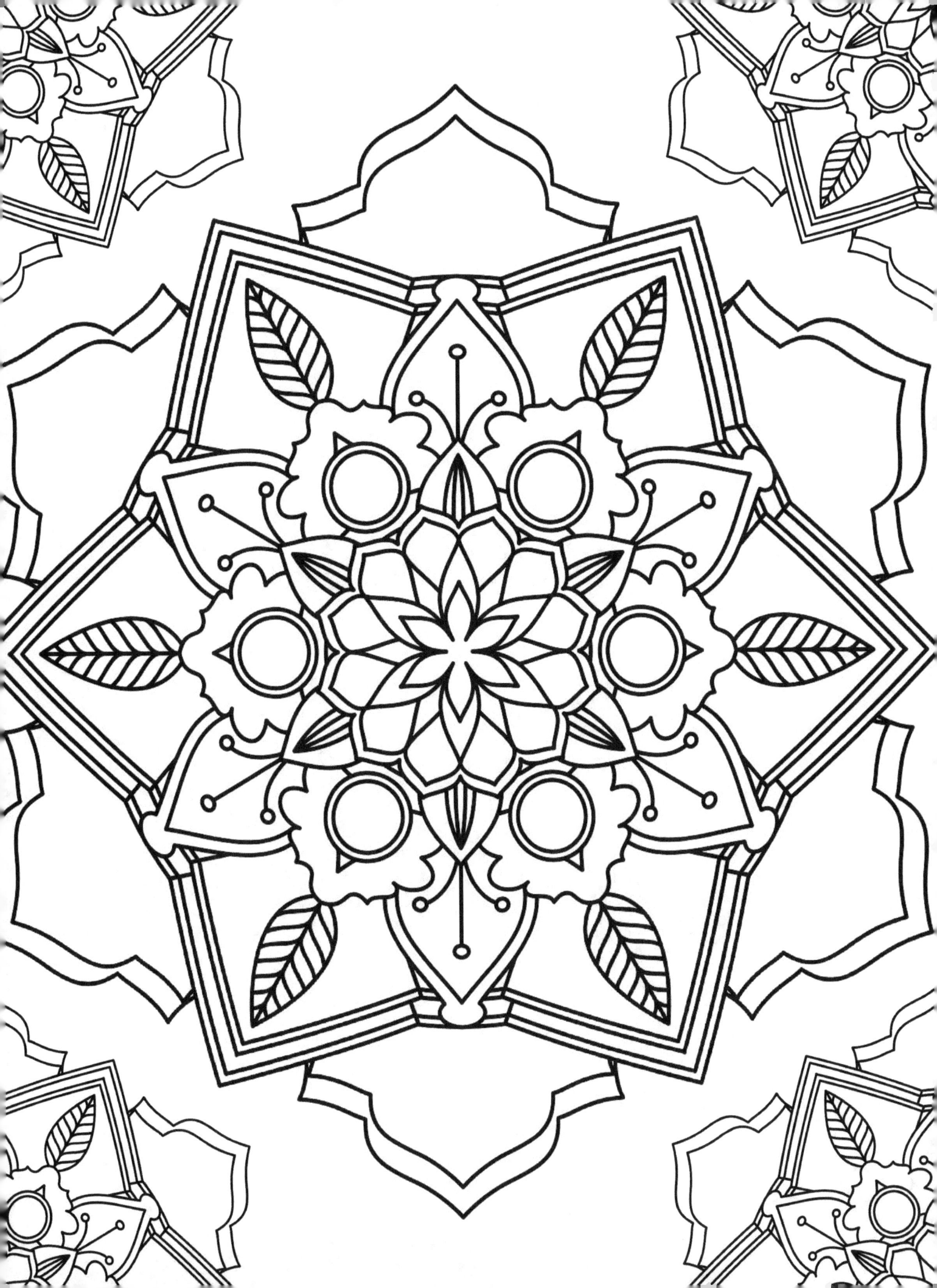

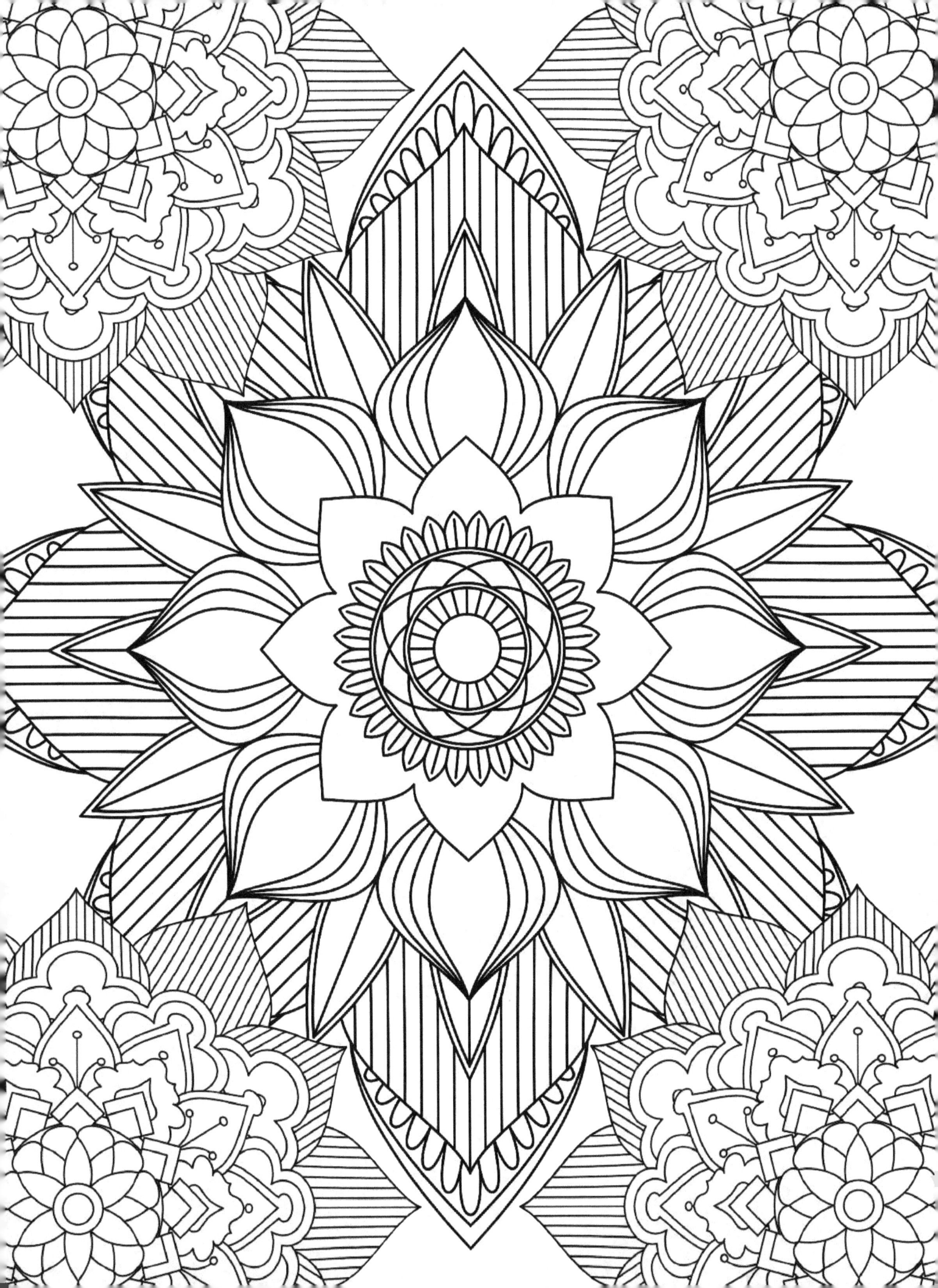

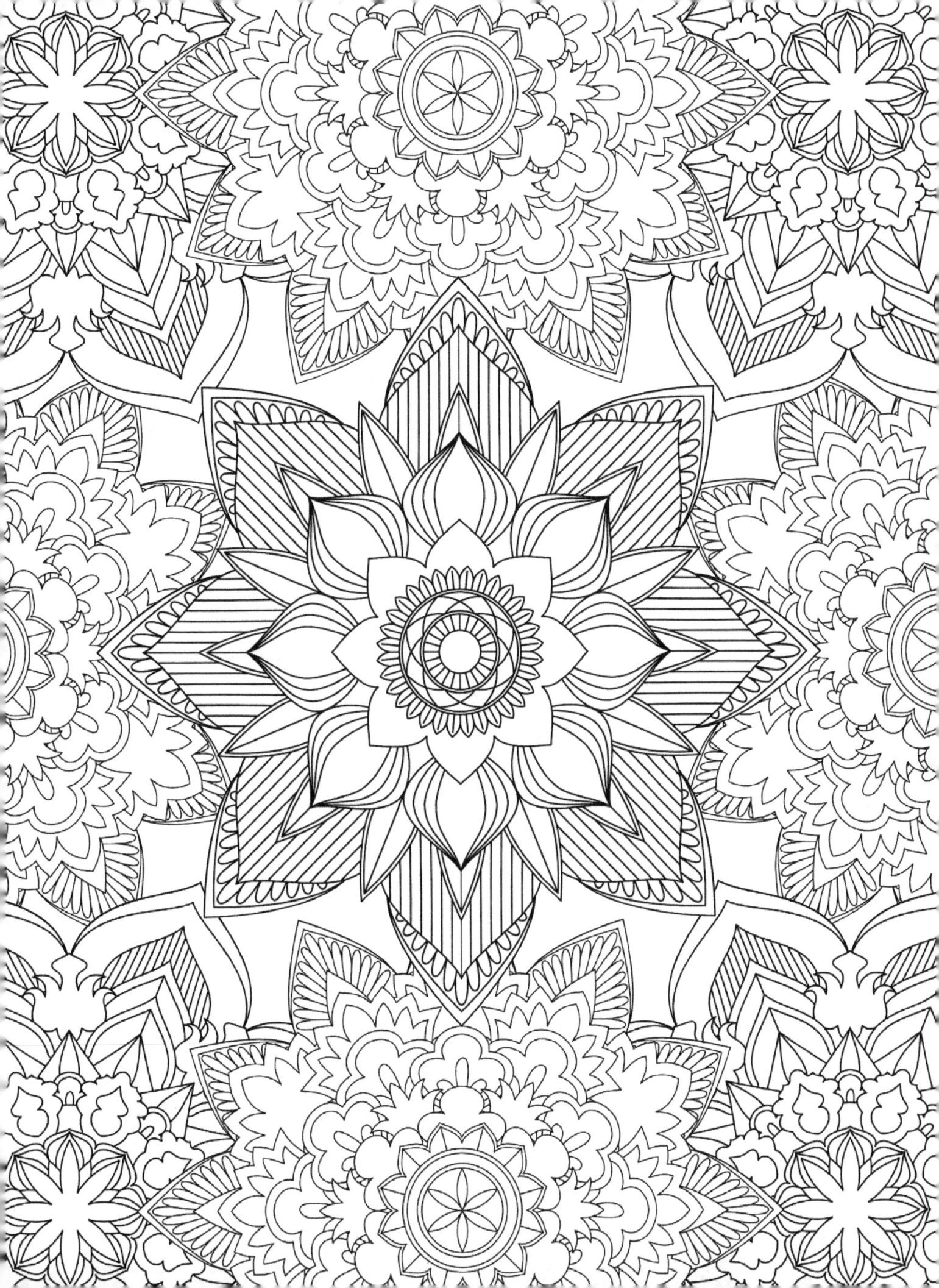

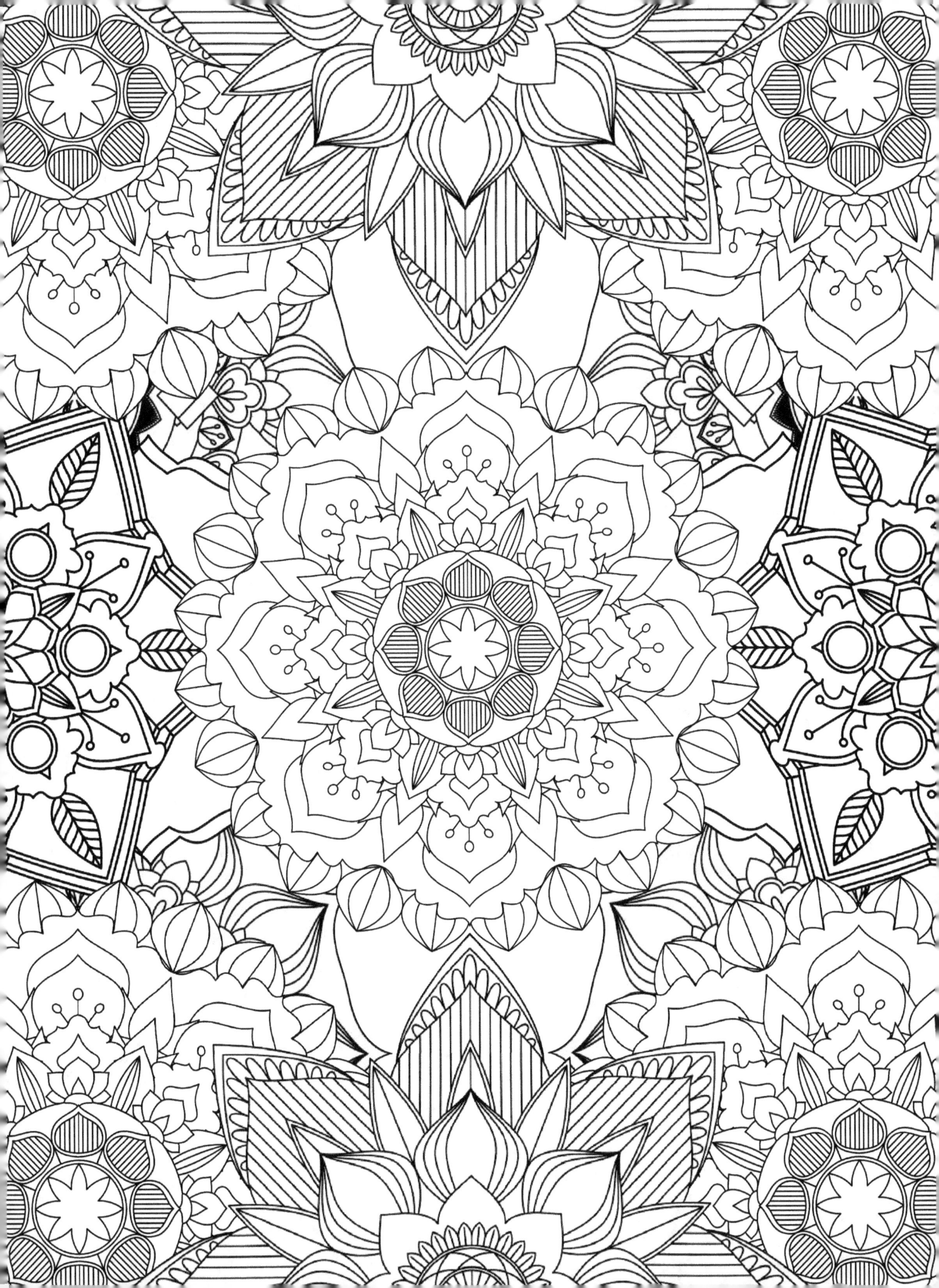

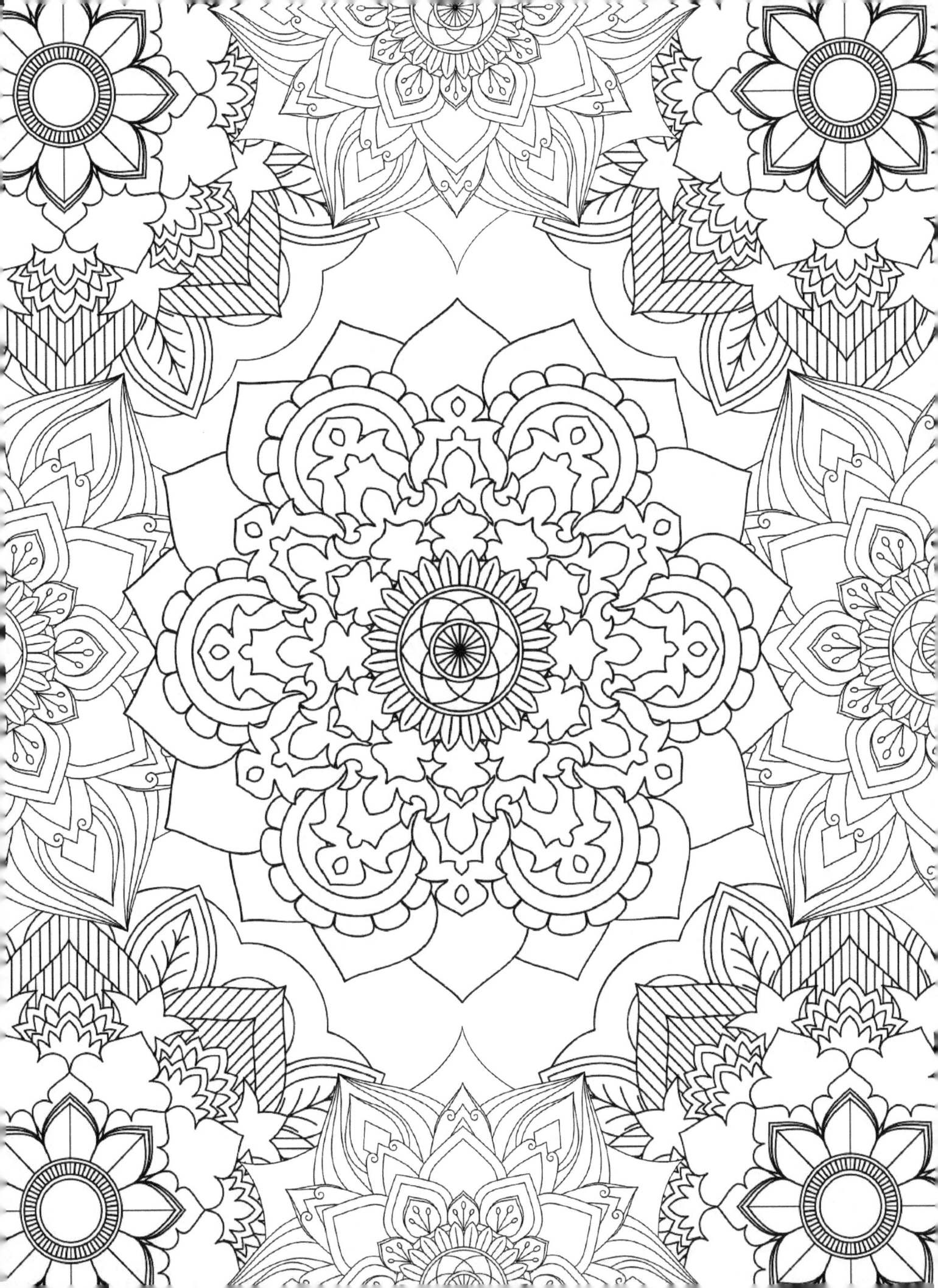

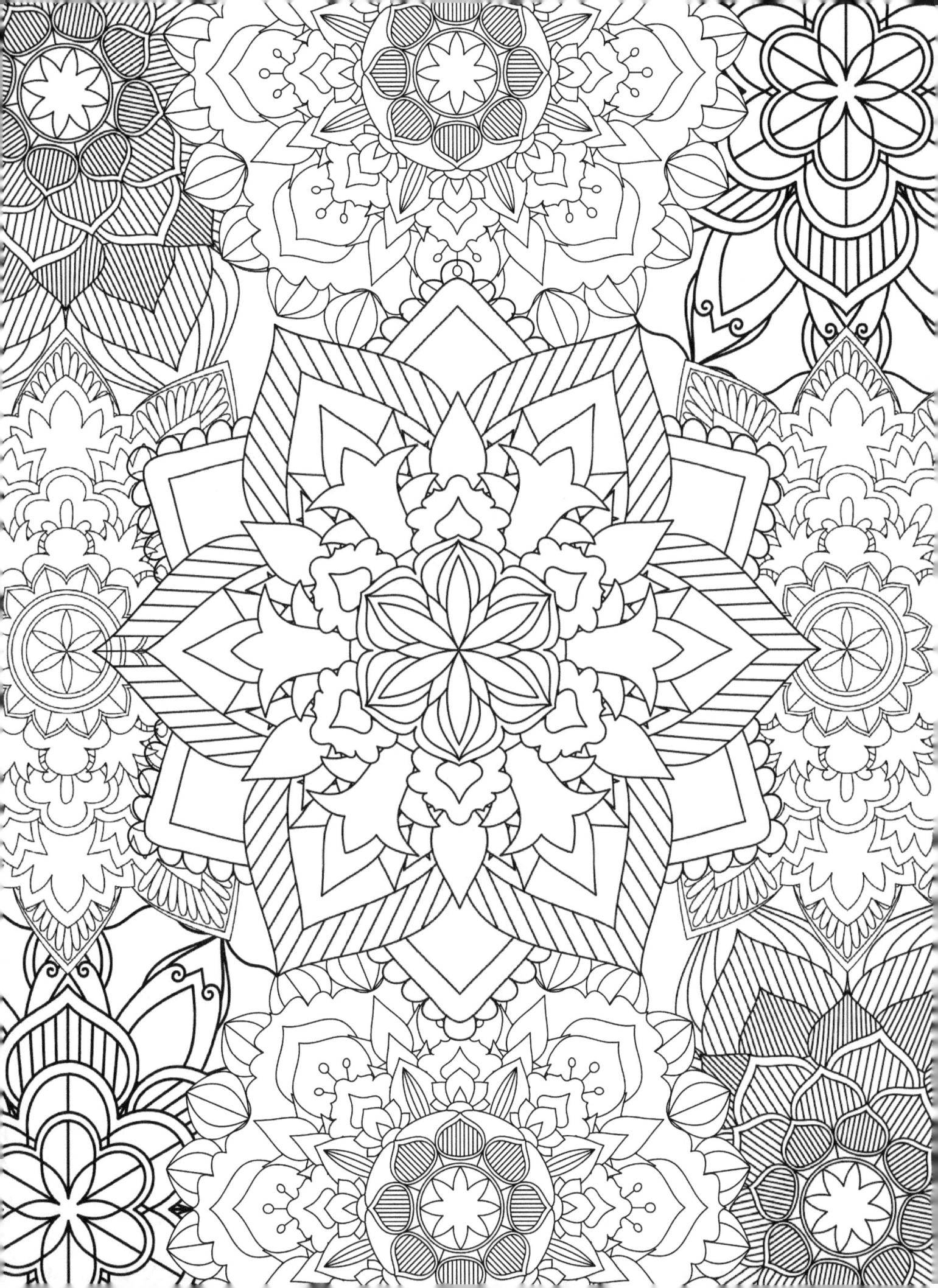

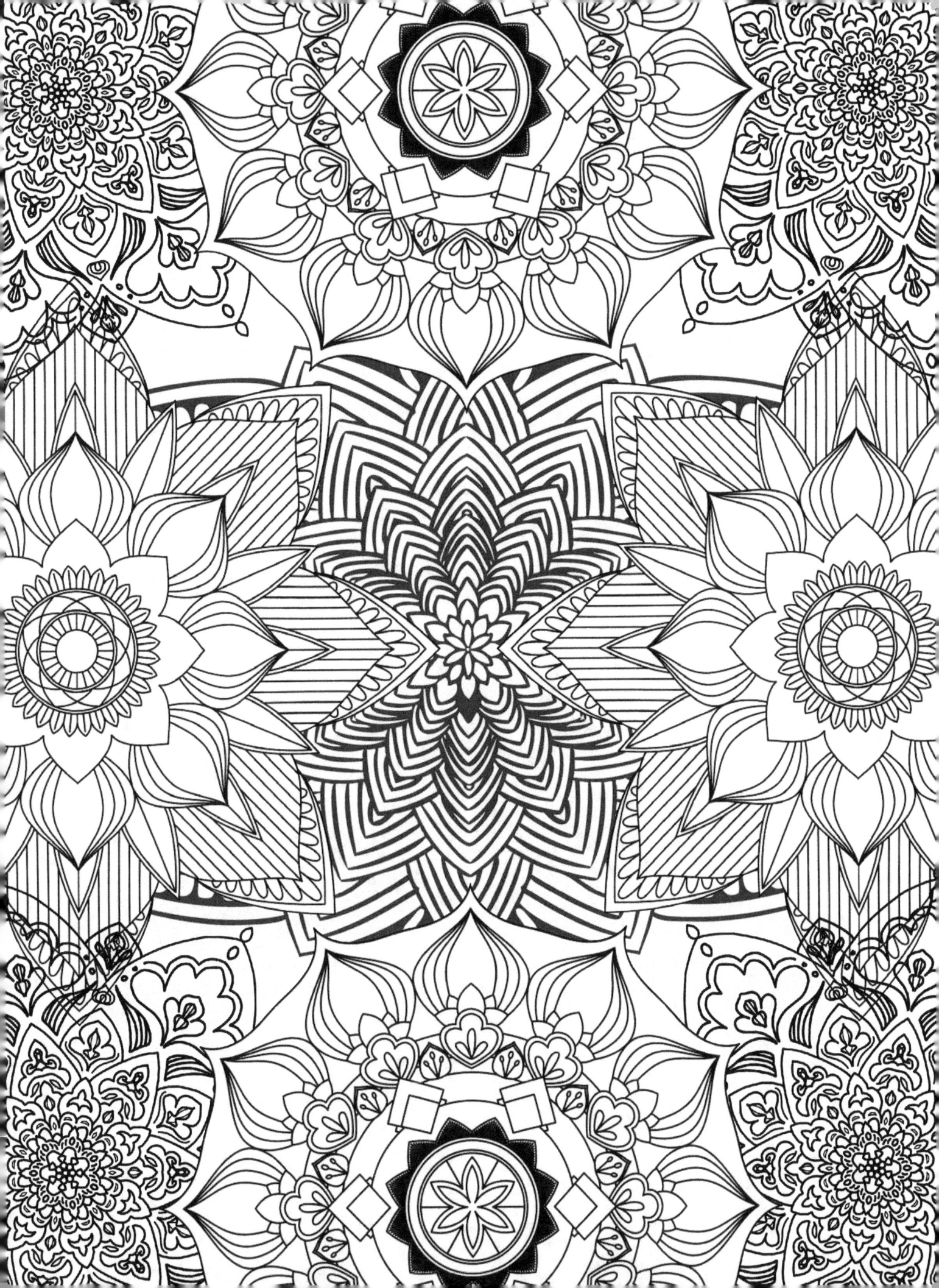

If you enjoyed this book, check out the coloring books available by

Sassy Scribblez

on Amazon.

www.ingramcontent.com/pod-product-compliance
Lightning Source LLC
Chambersburg PA
CBHW060427220526
45465CB00008B/3037